Kick It, Kim!

LEVEL 2

/k/

DECODABLES

BY jump!

Teaching Tips

Red Level 2

This book focuses on the phoneme **/k/**.

Before Reading

- Discuss the title. Ask readers what they think the book will be about.
- Sound out the words on page 3 together.

Read the Book

- Ask readers to use a finger to follow along with each word as it is read.
- Encourage readers to break down unfamiliar words into units of sound. Then, ask them to string the sounds together to create the words.
- Urge readers to point out when the focused phonics phoneme appears in the text.

After Reading

- Encourage children to reread the book independently or with a friend.
- Ask simple questions about the text to check for understanding. Have them find the pages that have the answers to your questions.

© 2024 Booklife Publishing
This edition is published by arrangement with Booklife Publishing.

North American adaptations © 2024 Jump!
5357 Penn Avenue South
Minneapolis, MN 55419
www.jumplibrary.com

Decodables by Jump! are published by Jump! Library.
All rights reserved. No part of this book may be reproduced in any form without written permission from the publisher.

Library of Congress Cataloging-in-Publication Data is available at www.loc.gov or upon request from the publisher.

ISBN: 979-8-88996-795-8 (hardcover)
ISBN: 979-8-88996-796-5 (paperback)
ISBN: 979-8-88996-797-2 (ebook)

Can you find these words in
the book?

kick

kid

Kim

Kim is a kid.

Kim

Kim can kick.

Kim kicks it.

Kim stops it.

Ken has it.

Ken

8

Ken does not kick it.

Can Kim kick it?

Kick it, Kim!

Can you say this sound and draw it with your finger?

Can you say this word and draw
it with your finger?

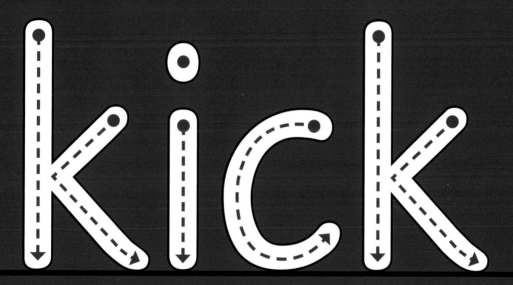

What other words do you know
that start with the letter /k/?

Practice reading the book again:

Kim is a kid.
Kim can kick.
Kim kicks it.
Kim stops it.
Ken has it.
Ken does not kick it.
Can Kim kick it?
Kick it, Kim!